Cairns

Cairns

Chris Hoffman

iUniverse, Inc.
Bloomington

Cairns

iUniverse books may be ordered through booksellers or by contacting:

iUniverse
1663 Liberty Drive
Bloomington, IN 47403
www.iuniverse.com
1-800-Authors (1-800-288-4677)

ISBN: 978-1-4759-8675-4 (sc)
ISBN: 978-1-4759-8676-1 (ebk)

Printed in the United States of America

iUniverse rev. date: 04/24/2013

Originally published by Orchard House Press (formerly Windstorm Creative)
First Edition December 2005
Second Edition September 2007

Chris Hoffman's poems capture both the spiritual essence and day-to-day nitty gritty of life in the canyons. Whether on raft or by foot, countless images emblazon light and shadow, sharply etched skylines and miniscule details, on our consciousness. His words and beautifully sculpted lines reverberate with passion and the intensity of his love for this magical place and space.

—Rick Medrick, E.D., Executive Director,
Outdoor Leadership Training Seminars and
Breaking Through Adventures

I take this book on the road with me, read the poems around sunrise and sunset, and feel both comforted and refreshed as I wander into wild places.

—Stephen R. Jones, author of *The Last Prairie*, and
Peterson Field Guide to the North American Prairie

A priest of desert and river, Chris Hoffman paints rich and satisfying imagery with his reverent pen.

—Cass Adams, editor of
*The Soul Unearthed: Celebrating Wildness and
Personal Renewal Through Nature*

Chris Hoffman does not write about things, he writes *in* things. Dwelling comes first. Poems happen afterwards.

This is not a poet whose narcissism stands in the way of his song. He is humbled by magic. For the sake of everything, he disappears. That's why his poetry is trustworthy. As with the ancients, he dispenses nectar freely because he doesn't know what else to do. This is his message: the wilder we get, the gentler we become.

Just by eating such words, filaments of luminosity might sprout from your skull. I recommend this book.

—Evan Hodkins, Director of the School of Alchemy.

For Susan,
once again and always

Singing that song protects the soul
and brings the soul home to its essence.

—*Skagit tradition of the Soul Song at birth*

Contents

Earth & Sky

Soul & Spirit

Love & Work

Pebbles

Acknowledgments

The author gratefully acknowledges the following publications in which some poems in this volume first appeared. "One Day" was originally published in *The Climbing Art*, Volume No. 28, 1995; "dandelions" and "lightning flash," in *Frogpond* Vol. XVII:1, Spring, 1994; "autumn aspen" in *Frogpond* Vol. XVII:3, Autumn, 1994; "Evening Sitting" in *Primary Point*, Volume 14, Number 1—Spring 1996; "At Cloud Pond" in *Appalachia*, June 2002; "Monhegan Island" in *Appalachia*, December 2004; "A Dream of the New Earth" in *PanGaia* #27, Spring, 2001; "Kenai Fjords" in *Sea-Kayaker*, February 1995, and in Adams, Cass (Ed.). *The Soul Unearthed* (New York: Tarcher/Putnam, 1996); "Saturday Morning" in the *The Christian Science Monitor*, May 14, 2003; "The Spark" in *EarthLight*, Spring 2003; "Medicine Bundle" in *EarthLight*, Spring 2005. Some poems in this volume originally appeared in the following chapbooks published by Yare Press: *Songs from Dream Canyon* (1985); *Map & Compass Work of the Spirit* (1987); *Humming to Lizards, Listening to Trees* (1990). Several of these poems benefited directly or indirectly from rigorous coaching by Parkman Howe. For inspiration and teaching I'm especially grateful to Robert Bly, Reg Saner, and William Meredith.

Earth & Sky

Put-In, Lee's Ferry
(Grand Canyon)

Twin sausage-shaped pontoons lashed
to a metal frame seemed an improbable craft at first.

Now the bulbous blunt ends of our boats
have been pressing the river beach for hours.
As the day has warmed
our ankles have grown cold in the water
with the hauling and lifting
of days of supplies in metal boxes and dry bags,
Again and again we've noticed the candy gloss
of little stones under the lucent water.
Now, after the strapping, the clipping with 'biners,
the checking and re-checking
that everything is here and secure;
after the safety talk,
the heavy boats tug at their lines
and we push off.

The river seizes us—
suddenly weightless and easy on the water—
and carries us with lilt and undulation.
Already the tamarisks at the put-in drift upstream,
on either side the cliffs begin to rise.
The air flutters desert-hot and river-cool;
and downstream where we're going,
through some aperture into a new life,
sequins of sunlight spangle and wink
on the rippling water.

Redwall Limestone
(Grand Canyon)

Redwall limestone,
sunburnt and swarthy
as the face of a Mongolian horseman.
Redwall limestone,
smooth and featured
as the palm of the hand.
Here you can trace the lifeline
and the line of Venus.
Redwall limestone,
huge blocks of it
chop down to the river's edge.
Manganese and iron oxides—
called "desert varnish"—
stain dark the broad and sweeping angles—
places like the heel of the hand
and where the thumb joins in.
Redwall limestone—
two palms of this
pressed together
in prayer or greeting,
but held apart by just this much
to let the river through.

River Trip to Bedrock
(Dolores River)

As the river carries you mile after mile
deeper into this desert canyon
all your clamoring wants and needs
begin to settle like silt in calm water.

Sinuous walls of Mesozoic sandstone,
slabbed and riven in huge buttery fractures, glow
at dawn and dusk with inner light.
The feathery tamarisks that fringe the river,
the pinon and juniper tucked in folds of slickrock,
the sweetly piping canyon wren,
the countless perfect little pebbles,
say: you are also this.

You pay attention, sparring
with the river, a martial artist
known to have occasionally gulped live people
and spit back their empty bodies.
You pull your oars, shove, watch your timing,
and feel against you the majesty
of the long fluid sinews, the supple cordage of water,
the power slashing at the rapids.

At camp, at night,
beneath a vast spray of stars
and the thinnest sliver of a moon
the rippling black water flutters
with shredded silver light.

As though awakening from a dream
you meet this place, called
here and now,
astonished.

Go to the Holy Desert

Go to the holy desert
at night and look at the sky,
where the stars extend beyond forgetting
in the emptying blackness deep and high.
They shine as clear as seeds of music
in the stillness of a prayer;
so many, they'll turn till numbering's numb
round the tail of the northern bear.
They accept everything that ever has been,
including your life. Lying there,
your body resolves to leather and bone,
and then to a grain of sand
on a shore between two mysterious oceans
where outward and inward expand.
Then secret beings crossing out and in
may brush you with their wings
and stir you to resonance with each moment
like a harp's quivering strings.
Go to the holy desert
at night and look at the sky,
where the twin cliffs above you open like eyelids
and you are the pupil of the infinite eye.

Silence on the Desert

Silence on the desert
is a diamond of the first water,
brilliantly clear;
where the only sound at all
is the tender pulse
whispering in your ear.

Mature, massy silence
aged like fine wine
in cellars of naked rock
makes of a single birdcall
a comma between eons.

Settling on that silence
as a compass needle on its jewel
you may pivot to your true direction.

At night the stars
wheeling in the utter deep
lean their huge weight on this silence
and—as diamond cleaves diamond—
split away
all you thought you were,
leaving you ever smaller
and more infinite.

Dusk

Pine pollen
softer than the dreams
of silkworms,
the sands of yellow beaches
deep in the woods . . .

Dusk settles into the canyon now;
formations of rock
take on the shapes of the night.
Close at hand this green ponderosa
has become a ladder of charcoal.
Above the ridge,
the crescent moon
fuzzes in a drift of pinks
      and rosy peach,
the sky almost drained of blue.

A lattice of cricket sounds
envelops the night.
Then a birdcall comes,
confident and liquid.

The moon returns
like a sail of brilliant ivory
rising over the dark sea.

The hoop of the night
passes around us
and we float into a new world.

On the San Juan River

Clear cool morning.
Blue sky. Deep, shadowed canyon.
The sun is starting to paint
the rim of the canyon
yellow ocher tattered with black.
Deep in the shadows still,
a tiny grey inflatable boat
nudges the slender beach
near a tumble of life jackets, ammo boxes, and dry bags—
little dabs of yellow, blue, and olive green
on a palette of sand.
The air quivers with the scent of tamarisk,
laced with the aroma of breakfast tea with milk.
Far downstream, a few clouds
are making fists.

Today's a day of swift sleek drifting
down the river.
No major rapids.
Long times no sound at all
but the faint slipping gurgle of the water.
Encyclopedias of stone
emerge from the slow tilt of the land,
stone that is not stone
but the congealed music
of the pipe organ of creation.

Listening closely you can hear
the resounding chords fading away.

A solitary great blue heron
standing in the shallows
examines the water like a posed question.
High up near the canyon rim
a huge roan- and cream-colored chunk
of the rock, sloughed-off and slid,
becomes a storytelling grandmother
with children of boulders
tugging at her skirts,
         clambering into her arms,
to hear how it all happened.
The heron flap flap flaps and glides
to another fishing place.

The river flows the color of strong tea with milk.
A flash flood gushing
from the severed artery of a side canyon
braids the water with ribbons of brown and dark red.
Sudden wind gusting
seems to push the river upstream,
blusters and billows the tarp
we huddle beneath.
We hold down its edges from inside—

knuckles wet from buckets of rain—
eat lunch with one hand,
and watch whole boulders
go under the rising river.

Wind and rain gone,
lazily drifting again,
lulled by the eloquent river
and the smooth warmth of the afternoon,
we slowly enter
the pith of tranquility.
Mild breeze.
Knife-winged swallows deftly
whittle the air.
Later, a flock of green-winged teal
fly arpeggios
of curvature and felicity.

Calm evening.
Camp. Supper.
After the last ammo box snaps shut
with a solid clank:
deep silence again
and the sure, subtle swish of the water.
We fall asleep listening

to the whiskery electric squeaks of bats,
and examining
the crystal-beaded black black beauty
of the nighttime desert sky.

The mirror of dreams
splinters
with a crack of branched fire.
Struck awake
in total blackness
we hear the whole of space
crumpling around us.
Then: flashes of lightning,
canyon walls volley the thunder.

In this moment,
each breath tasting so delicious,
we crawl into the tent
and receive the benedictions
of the mild, fitful rain.

At Cloud Pond

A glittering flake of sky nestles here
in the cup of the mountainside.

After hiking so far alone
nowhere to be but here.

I swim fully naked in clear water,
hugging a slippery floating tree trunk.

In the lean-to, dry, I eat a small supper.
With the storm, astonishing thunder.

Cold rain pelts, subsides. One by one
across the pond pines step out of the mist.

One Day

I walked with my friend
along the high spine of the mountains—
that beautiful bitter edge—
all the clouds and the round world
now lower than my feet.
I should have known better—
stepping down the yielding froth
of early-season snow
as clean as sugar.
I heard the thunder first
and wondered, but everything began
the terrible jiggling—
everything, I say:
the whole locomotive of winter—
nothing solid
but a maw of snow
sucking my feet.
"This is it," I thought;
and I watched,
each moment expecting
Now? Or now?
The sky sunk upward.
Then: mountains of silence.

I could see some bleary crystalled light;
my right forearm waved in the air.
Years later I learned
my friend had looked
and looked
and looked
and almost left
but looked again.
I remember my one free hand
clawing for my nose.
I remember calling out.

Getting down from there to timberline
was larceny: stealing elevation
from the jaws of avalanches.
One pair of skis between us now.
Wet and cold.
No trail. And losing daylight.
We crashed through willow thickets
knee-deep in snow,
and found the road
just before we would have lost
our hands in front of us to darkness.

Though, like most of us,
I think I know what happens next
from day to day,
sometimes a moment blazes like a diamond
and everything is as it is
and holy,
swaying from a dark stem.

Backpacking, Mt. Zirkel Wilderness

After the dust of the trail
the weight of the pack rests
on the ample ground.

Sitting back against the cushion
of sleeping bag in stuff sack,
look out over the vast house of the winds,
the enormous crags that drop
to fields of miniature boulders,
the tiny lakes glittering in green meadows,
the undulant forest of spruce that robes the rock bones,
where each spray of new needles
is pushing off its little varnished cap,
and far in the distance
the wide world bending away.

Bees thrum in the stillness,
busy pollinating Old-Man-Of-The-Mountain.
A few dried apricots
and a long drink of lukewarm water
make a feast.

San Rafael

We take the place of water in the desert—
pouring down a slot canyon
in the dry season, so narrow
in places you can easily touch both walls
at once, hands on fine grit sandstone,
salmon colored or dirty cream,
water-smoothed, scooped and fluted
fleshy rock. We edge down ledges
under overhangs, squeeze down chutes
and clamber over chock stones the size of Buicks.
Underfoot—the crunch of dry gravel,
the push of sand, the scrape of boots on rock;
high overhead the sky
is a winding ribbon of blue.

Rest for a moment where the canyon
widens a bit. Observe where the walls
are pitted in huge swatches of wind-carved cavities
like a weirdly drooping honeycomb. At night
a candle in each of these niches
would make a galaxy.

Peel away all you think about this world;
peel away what you think about this moment.
Now is not like that.

Everything fits together—our exertion,
the multitudinous shapes of rock,
the solitude, our inner lives, our water bottles,
the grey-brown dormant brush, the specks of vivid green.
Sweet medicine of beauty, seeping in,
begins to heal our broken places,
re-weaves us in the web of life.

Because I am comfortable, because
I have food, water, clothing, and sunscreen,
because I have a car with which to drive back to camp
and a sleeping bag there, and a tent,
and more food, and money to pay for gas
to drive back home, with a house there
and heat and clean water on tap
and indoor plumbing and good work
to pay for it all and skills and health
and friends and family,
I can speak of this intimate slot in the earth
and of its wild beauty. Who can say
we are not inconceivably interconnected?
Pick at any thread and the whole
weaving would unravel.

—As in this present war.
The shopkeeper stands in front
of his bombed and burned-out shop,
his neighbors, his customers, his children carried off
in bloody stretchers improvised from blankets.
He says, "We were just trying to earn our living.
What do they want from us? Now
it is gone, all gone."

The threads are blown apart,
the web of life is bleeding.
A galaxy of candles could not heal his loss
nor any other suffering
in this suffering world.

And yet, and yet . . .
healing, when it comes at all,
flows from the source of beauty.
So we must honor every instance,
every taste of being wholly intimate as one with life,
and nourish that, and carry it like a precious flame
and share it wick to wick
until the web is mended,
shining like a galaxy of candles.

Morning, River Camp
(Desolation and Gray Canyons, Green River)

It is early yet—the hour of the gray dawn.
All night we have slept on the smooth
    thigh of the sand.
Our first waking breath is of air scrubbed
clean by sage and sun, tamarisks and swift water.
Just upstream, the rapids
are still scouring the silence. The river
continues its long, gathering slide.

In the gray dawn the river is dull
as are the canyon walls, while the high gap
of sky floods with luminous blue.
A bird proclaims himself; and then another.
Rising sunlight slants slowly down across cliffs
of ancient lake bed sediment, kindling colors on its way—
tawny rock with horizontal bands of reddish brown,
then talus slopes verdigris with sagebrush,
tufted with juniper green. The river's ripples
play with light now, pushing polished patches
of blue sky, roan cliff, and green-leafed cottonwood.

What a good thing it is to wake every day,
and how soon our minds are ordinarily clouded.
Here, like brother canyon wren and sister whip snake,
we always awaken to the first day. This earth
opens the shutters of our inner house
so the one who is always present
can flow through us into the world.

Psalm

I give my bones to the rocks;
The rocks give my bones to me.
I give my flesh to the soil;
The soil gives my flesh to me.
I give my blood to the ocean;
The ocean gives my blood to me.
I give my veins to the rivers;
The rivers give my veins to me.
I give my heart to the sun;
The sun gives my heart to me.
I give my hair to the grass;
The grass gives my hair to me.
I give my tongue to the brook;
The brook gives my tongue to me.
I give my spine to the tree;
The tree gives my spine to me.
I give my dance to the deer;
The deer gives my dance to me.
I give my tears to the dew;
The dew gives my tears to me.
I give my growl to the bear;
The bear gives my growl to me.
I give my dreams to the moon;
The moon gives my dreams to me.
I give my song to the coyote;

The coyote gives my song to me.
I give my sight to the hawk;
The hawk gives my sight to me.
I give my touch to the spider;
The spider gives my touch to me.
I give my bones to the rocks;
The rocks give my bones to me.

I hear a voice
from every stone
calling me, calling me—
The earth is my body,
I shall not want.

Delicate Arch, Utah

Hiking to see for ourselves, we learn
once again why pilgrims journey by walking.
The steady rhythm of left and right
reassures us. And the gravel of the trail
becomes those places in our minds
we keep climbing over
and over again.

The work of the walking
is our offering,
and our purification
as, step by step,
we lift the questing in our hearts
closer to the source of wonder.
Irrelevancies slide away like sweat.
The walking reminds us of balance,
and the sheer drop-off by the edge of the trail
is our own death walking beside us.

We lift our expectancy like an empty plate;
and abundance of beauty
fills it again and again.
This world is so huge,
and our place in it so precise.

Eventually there is nothing but
walking and wondering.
Climbing higher with the other pilgrims
and with a sense of all the tribes returning
to the place of creation,
we round a bend, and there—
an impossible leap of stone,
a petrified gasp of wonder,
orange-red, arcing through the bluest desert sky,
a stone mudra, gathering light,
parabolic angel bones
framing distant snowy peaks.

All the living beings of this earth
pass under the pubic arch
of our common mother.
And she is right here.
True to her nature,
she lets no one depart empty—
Through the great opening
comes a whisper of blessing
or a glimpse that opens
the eyes of the eyes.

We know that when we turn
the trail will lead us back
into our daily lives, walking,
striving for balance,
practicing the rhythm of left and right,
but touching a thread
that leads through the eye of the needle.

Monhegan Island

Spruce boughs are bouncing
high on the headlands.

A salt wind off the North Atlantic
slams wave after wave on the solid shore.

Out on the wrinkling, wallowing water
windrows of foam tumble and scud.

The tide-swollen ocean claws relentlessly higher
over the brown mass of knotted wrack, over

the rockweed with its pimply bladders,
crashes and splays on knuckles of primeval granite.

In the chunk and crush
so many colors of white—rough cream, fluent

snow, and over the elegant fins of curling
green, webs of antique lacework, sliding.

Just above the spray line a solitary
gull on dry rock lowers his weight,
tucks his head, pushes into the wind.

High beyond the reach of tides, a storm-
tossed lobster pot, its strong green wires mangled,
wobbles in the gusts.

Aurora Borealis, Summer

Awake again
at midnight, when late sunset lingers
underneath the pole star—
the great dipper swung high in blackness—
huge streaks of pale light
sweep across the sky, leaning northward—
light like visible music,
as though some hand had made a harp of the galaxy
and was now striking unfathomable resonances,
sustained and shimmering chords—
an enormous flower of the night
unfurling petals of pale electric greens and yellows.

Some say we enter and leave this body
through the northern door
at the crown of the head
where something else precipitates into *me*
and some time later flies out again.
I think of the tremendous velocity of that passage
and of how it must surround us
with visible music.

This Evening
(Canyonlands)

This evening, the desert wind
riffles the gorgeous tail of the coyote
as she lies dead
with flies feeding on the horrible
tissue from her eye socket.

Around her: far reaches of sage,
rice grass, black brush, distant
muscular naked flanks of slickrock,
immense phalluses and mounds,
quickly relinquishing their hoarded solar heat
to the air. The sky's blue dissolving
reveals the infinite black nothing
we float in, seeded with star beings.

How was this coyote's dying?
Did she think of her pups
or remember the taste of mouse;
Did she shrink into her pain?
Or was she able to abandon coyote
and wholly stream back to the sourceless source?
What image did she choose
as the doorway for this passage?
Who smiled on her with perfect love
as we would someone smile on us?

Alone,
in the resounding silence of the desert night
what use is it to pretend?
The rocks say: much older.
The sky says: much bigger.
The four-wing saltbush says:
able to thrive on little water.
What can we offer
as our own true nature?

Our lives are like the colorful threads
of a patterned blanket.
And we see only one side of the weaving
where the thread emerges, runs, and disappears.
The coyote has disappeared.
We shall disappear.

The best we can do
is take care of this moment,
and this one . . . and this.
A great emptiness unfolds
like a beautiful paper fan
painted with all that is.

The Lathe of the Wind
(Canyonlands)

Turned
on the lathe of the wind,
bowls, towers, spires,
sentinels, ridges, fins
become these desert canyons,
rough-sawed by cloudburst runoff
through upthrust layered rock
of dune and ancient seabed:
patiently rasped
by threadlike seasonal creeks
that glitter in their seasons.
Alarmingly beautiful!
Red and cream and tan
and yellow-orange sandstone,
ridged and cupped
as the folds of the ear,
dwarf
the sparse and dark green Utah juniper
as though the stone had grown
by deep listening to stars.

Our ancestors here, long ago,
husked the green dress
for the golden body of the woman of corn.

Now their few, ruining granaries
tucked in cracked cliffs
watch with questioning eyes
when we come, in solitary ones and twos,
to this place of deep listening.

Clouds move
and fingers of sunlight play
over the keyboard of the rocks.
Sometimes the humming of insects
carries gently across the canyon.
Most times, no sound at all
when the wind dies down.
And the world as the bride of the wide sky
shines wide with brightness.
This raw and elemental beauty
dries up our inner chatter
until the whole of creation floats
on the surface of breathing.
Listen.
Who is living this?
The walls of the small mind fall away
as, alone, luminous, and empty,
we traverse the footprint of the great mystery.

Kenai Fjords

This little kayak gives me an ocean for legs.
I stand where the pelagic sea birds float
and slide beside sleeping otters
rocking in their big bay cradle.
My kayak's prow skims through the water
parting a vee as delicate as a raindrop's ripple,
gracefully tracing fine and vanishing calligraphy,
sensitive and eager as a lover's first intimate touch.
I will go with my kayak to the place of glaciers,
to where the ice age crouches by the ocean,
probing with thick fingers of ice,
stilling its chill breath
and hoping for a long, cold winter.

I glide past the incessant gnawing of ocean at cliffs,
past the slack and bloom of wavelets plashing
on beaches cobbled with black stones.
Braided streams like long lace
from the white linen tablecloth of icefields
     and snowfields
plunge reckless and tangled in their abundance
down steep verdant slopes—
numberless unnamed waterfalls pounding and roaring.
Flurries of wary puffins whack the water
in their take-off runs.
Orange beaks make bright wedges

in a misty grey-green grey-blue grey-grey world.
Here are the shores where the bear's tongue tastes
blueberry and sweet red cloudberry by multitudes—
taut sacks bursting in wild explosions of flavor;
Here is where the bear's paw
pulls miraculous salmon from the thronging streams.
A bald eagle flies to its nest, sculpting the air with its wings;
Mew gulls and kittiwakes swoop and pluck at the water;
An arctic tern hovers over the beach, wheeling and crying;
In the distance, rugged mountains in three shades of grey
kneel into the sea.

O to go buoyant on the liquid muscle of the sea
and to be so small in this immensity, but present
        and alive!
In my speck of kayak
I balance on the gliding swell and dancing chop
and watch the crystal beads that fallen raindrops make
before the ocean sucks them in.
I reach with my paddle and push my boat forward
and breathe with the rhythm of sliding along.
The ocean supports me and welcomes my paddle
and I move like a swimmer immersed in a song.
I move like a swimmer, I move like a swimmer,
and I move like a swimmer immersed in a song.
To be here this way is something
        delicious and forbidden—
like being in a warm safe night, outdoors and naked.

In this little kayak I glide towards the glacier;
and I hear the tomb of ancient winters
    slowly speaking—
muttered booms cushioned by the silence
    of deepening cold.
Seals slide into the water and simply watch—
scores of grey-headed periscopes with soft eyes.
I pass islands of ice that sometimes pop and crackle
    as they melt.
The water is milky blue-grey and barely salty;
and through the kayak it drinks the heat from my body.
The wall of ice grows and grows taller and taller,
wider and wider as I drift closer.
It is white and dirty black
and the piercingly impossible edge of blue—
a barrier of grotesquely beautiful shapes
    hundreds of feet high
and hundreds hundreds wide.
A still and terrifying calmness descends on my soul
in the expanse of this unseen presence.
A young sandhill crane, poised
    in single-pointed weight,
turns and graciously walks away.
This world in its rawness is ever sacred.

Go There

Go there
for the nothing that is there.

You may find the lakes,
minted from sunlight
or moody in their mists and veils.

You may creep, small and warily,
under the tall suspended pounce
of cliffs.

You may stagger ankle-deep
through the juicy green
of mountain meadows,
dazzled by their embroidered robes
of white and yellow flowers.

Your fingers may feel
the specific grittiness of this rock.

You may stand up under the stars
wearing nothing but starlight.

All you behold
is the universe looking at you.

The wide sweep of the tundra,
the pine trees stooped by the wind,
the sharp peaks, the falls of tumbling water—
the whole land hums the tunes
of sacred geometry.

Go there opening the miracle
like a swimmer parting the water.

There, where gravity is the first teacher,
you push the earth away with each step,
with each step you return.
Slowly you discover

you fill your place
as water fills a cup
as one hand greets another.

Each part of this universe
reaches out invisible arms
anticipating your love.

Go there for the nothing you are.
The clenched bubble of separate identity
rises to the surface
and, with a little sparkle,
relaxes open.

A Dream of the New Earth

Once upon a time
the earth will be new again,
scars healed, roads narrowed,
all life flourishing,
clear-cuts lush with old growth
sustainably harvested,
rivers pure to drink from,
the birds come back, flashing
and speckled fish thronging the seas,
the minefields will be cleared,
the radioactivity gone,
no more stabbings or beatings
or wrongful tears in the night;
the work of humans
will be a few things beautifully made,
humble and fit,
with music, jokes, ceremony,
poetry, and dance in endless abundance
in place of a vomit of stuff
reeking of obsession and bound for the landfill,
humankind scaled back, its factories and cities
no longer a plague
that pimples and blisters the landscape
but a string of jewels
on the body of the earth,
the air fit to breathe again

simple silence available
and billions of stars at night.
O may we weave ourselves
into the fabric of life
and truly feel the path,
smooth or rocky, beneath our feet,
and be worthy of this passage,
long or short,
between the two doorways
where naked we enter
and naked we depart.

The Spark

Sometimes
when you round a bend
or come over a crest
the word you use for divinity
will wake in your heart and fly
through your mouth urgently
out into the universe.

This is the spark
that shows your own life
has struck against the great life
like flint on steel.

There will be a certain clarity
of space, with every mountain range,
every tree, every blade of grass,
every glistening water droplet or grain of sand
distinct
yet wedded at the core.

Don't cling to this experience.
Don't put your bread on the shelf
so you can admire it.
Eat it fresh.
Digest it.
Let it become who you are.

Soul & Spirit

Medicine Bundle

It may start with a stone
on the ground that draws
your eye and then your hand.
Holding it, you feel better.
It reminds you of something.
In the room of the heart
where your soul sits
hangs a sacred object
that is part of who you are
and why you are here.

Deep in the night, or when you are sick
or feeling lost, you unwrap the stone
from its swaddling of cloth or leather or birch bark
and sit in that heart room
rediscovering your feet and your true direction.

When you are doing hard inner work
something else begins to appear
on the curving wall of that inner room,
something you don't recognize until
someone gives you a bead
or a bird leaves you a feather
or you find a pin with wings in the gutter.

The new object, blessed and carefully
wrapped, joins your bundle.
Slowly the encircling blank wall fills
with what was meant to be there—
experience and insight as constellations
of simple precious things.

From the four directions
animal beings enter and leave
carrying greetings, messages.
When we feed them, they feed us.

In the floor of the heart room
a hole reaches down to the center
of the universe. Descend
to retrieve the dragon's teeth
as balls of sap from a lightning-blasted tree.
They join your bundle.

From these moist depths also
dream images from the unhealed side
become the clay for your pottery,
the pigment for your paint,
the tones for your music,
the gestures for your dance,
the images for your poems,
the juice for your life.

A piece of this darkness
goes into your bundle also.

From the floor of this room
a ladder ascends through a hole in the roof
and disappears among the clouds.
This is where the smoke of your incense
rises carrying your prayers
as you sit with your bundle
of little stones, twigs, seeds,
beads, bones, feathers, and bits of metal—
the physical presence
of the mysterious holy.

So praise and defend
the bat and her kin
and the bristlecone pine,
the sagebrush lizard with his blue bib,
the coral reef swirling with life,
nighthawk, badger, the four mountains,
and the worm awaiting under your feet.

Remember: your ancestors hoped for your life;
and everyone you meet has a heart room,
unused and dusty though it may be.
We journey outward to give attention
to the beauty of the world.
When it awakens our inner silence
we are alive with listening.

Evening Sitting

At the mouth of this little cave,
a pile of three stones
makes a Buddha;
the smoke from a pinch of herbs
curls gracefully.
A single candle,
      a cup of water,
            the night drifts in . . . .
Somewhere in the deeper caves of sleep
a female kestrel nestles in my hair,
brushing with soft feathers,
and says,
"She loves us all."
Later
the boulder
      at the mouth of the cave
blushes
      with the first kiss of dawn.
Then the rich man from the east
drenches the tree tips
with yellow gold.

To Walk

To walk.
To wake in the morning
and thread through the maze
of daily routines,
with a sense
like a hand on the banister,
and then
with a pouch of blue corn meal
tucked in shirt pocket
simply
to walk,
for a moment away
from the household,
slowly,
to where the trees
continue their dialog with earth
about water.
To walk,
and do the labor of devotion
with the legs and the feet,
simply
to walk,
such balance
an amazing grace,
freely to meet the air,

the bird song,
the lengthening afternoon,
the well-walked path
and then the secret one,
climbing slightly
to a much-loved place,
simple, really: a cleft in the rocks.
To walk there,
pretending nothing,
just to feel the presence
like clear spring water
against the lips of your soul.
To walk
to say some prayers with cornmeal
and finding there
your long-forgotten prayerstick,
to see the notch
your knife had made,
to see the perfect feathers
now gone to mouse-food
and wrapping-yarn faded grey—
for a moment,
for a moment
the other you are

lets itself be glimpsed
as two, powerful birds—
one on either side—
who have been flying beside you
all these days and nights.

The Spirit of the Great Bear

When the spirit of the Great Bear
entered my body
I felt myself upright, ambling
with the gait of one who
could go much faster on all fours.
When the spirit of the Great Bear
entered my body
I raised my paws in supplication
and heard the stars singing.
When the spirit of the Great Bear
entered my body
we hiked out of this world;
realms beyond realms flashed by with every
    shimmering step;
I felt myself be both male and female at the same time.
In a sacred manner we walked
between the spread invisible legs of Mother Night.
This Bear's paws parted the veil
of the original sound,
and the silence beyond—
    a golden abundant emptiness—
was given as water to drink.

When the spirit of the Great Bear
entered my body
I saw more than I can understand,
but I can tell you
Destiny wears a lover's face.

Room Full of Moons

I saw a room full of moons,
full and ripe, like alabaster fruit,
brilliant in the black enamel of the night.
I saw a room full of moons.
It was an upstairs room,
an attic where the high ceiling
was a sky full of moons,
where black and white mingled fiercely,
where globes of ivory-and-bone-light glowed
in the black intensity of night.
I saw a room full of moons—
It was a spacious, secret place
in an old house
where antique moons clustered
like grapes swollen with juice
among the black leaves of the sky.
I saw a room full of moons
where the walls and ceiling were a sky
that was as black
as the sea of mysterious departure.
It was a secret room in a small house
but the air was so sweet there
and the moons so many and the sky so full of beauty
that I knew this room
was a porch of the infinite.

Courtship of Bald Eagles

I stroke the air that strokes you.
You tip your wings
as I begin to bank.
Together we embrace a space
wider than all my loneliness.

Thermal of my soul,
as we winnow these winds together,
so unison in our delight,
you make me light enough
to preen the down of rainbows;
and the wide world below
glitters with detail
that I had never seen.

When I feel your wings
thrusting lift into mine,
whole skies open within me.
To fly with you is all I ever want,
Until we shudder, rising
in the golden talons of the sun.

How It Happens

It's an old story: Dusk
in the land between now and then.
The sweet breath of evening
settles into the desert canyon.

Clean now as a river cobble
after songs and prayers in the womb
of the sweat lodge,
sit with the wise ones
listening to clear speech, clear silences.

Grandfather sends you out into the night
for water. "Get it from upstream
on the river," he says. He says,
"I've been with the river all of my life."

The river is surprisingly warm
in the cool night air. Squatting by clear water
with your gourd, canteen, or plastic bottle
you turn and see how far alone you have come
into the night, really dark now, no moon.

You hear your own breathing, then
strange sounds coming closer.
From out of the inner reaches of the night
a bird or animal appears, sits beside you,
its eyes closed, looking you over from within.

It reaches deeply, down
through the floor of your consciousness
all the way to the river of living water.
You return with the unforgettable taste.

Prayer

I pray to the one who knows me fully,
the wisdom veiled in my confusion,
the calm within my desires,
the one who never will condemn or abandon me,
who holds my opposites with two hands
    cupped together,
who comes as a white owl, a black bear,
a council of elders in my dreams,
as the first breath in the morning,
as the last kiss goodnight,
for whose sake I sit quietly
to hear the soft plash of wavelets on the lake shore,
and for whom I hike to be able to witness
    pine and aspen,
green and gold in autumn,
draping their kilt over the hips of the mountains,
to the one who dwells in the taste of water,
who wells up now and now and now,
who considers my life sacred,
the one whom I long for
and who, through my longing,
sweeps me into the great dance.

After Reading Meister Eckhart

When next you open a door,
notice how the hinge stays still
yet guides and anchors the smooth
and sweeping arc into the world.

Your own arc in the world—
all your movement from birth
to death—is likewise anchored
and guided at a deep, still place.

The leaf falling from the tree in autumn
flutters and glides in its descent;
the stone continues its smooth
sinking into the pond; and you, too,

in dream or vision go down
into the otherworld—past your
wish-fulfillment, past the images that scare
you, past their hooks and teeth.

Your inner companion, who appears
in many forms, will guide you to a hermitage
called the true you, where your hinge is,
and touch your brow with pigment
opening your core's clear eye.

What you see there cannot be named,
but only hinted at with healing water,
a sprouting seed, a golden flame.
Looking up and out you see the bright
threads that weave everything together.

Here is where the breath you breathe
touches the life that breathes your breath.
From here, all your own peculiarities
are simply ways for manifesting
the deep and good unsayable
that guides and anchors your arc.

Two Musicians
(from an old story)

When Han played,
sensate truth
he plucked like ripe fruit
from his strings.
When he played of mountains
there were mountains;
and when he sang of spring
flowers bloomed in his mouth.

When Lu listened
he bit to the core.
Where others heard
widening ripples,
Lu saw even the frog
hop in the pond.

One person listens,
the other sings.
When Lu the listener died,
Han cut his strings.

At the Well

When I stand at the well
with my beloved beyond name
all the parts of my life arrive
like guests to a wedding.
None will be kept away.
My brilliant times
and my failures of truth,
my selfishness, and the brief moments of grace,
one by one step into the circle.
Suddenly the pattern is clear—
the symmetry
and the colors like glass on fire,
the subtlety of the dark designs
transfigured now
and soft as the fur under the mouse's belly.
Nothing to do now
but, in every thought and action,
offer water.

Bear

When the black bear crawled out of my dream
last night and into my bed
and wrapped his huge furry paws around me
I felt very safe. His being there said
we are always climbing the mountains
that consist of darkness; the water
is always clearer than we imagine;
and the cave out of which we both
have crawled, opens and opens and opens . . .

Biwa
("bee-wah")

Biwa is the drum.
Biwa is the drum.
Biwa.
Biwa told me.
Biwa is the drum.
Biwa carries dreamers.
Biwa guards the door.
Biwa's hip thickens.
Biwa cradles the baby's head
when its body is being pushed out.
Biwa pushes.
Biwa is the drum.
Biwa is the drum
Biwa knows.
Biwa.
Biwa speaks out in the dusk.
Biwa speaks out in the jungle.
Biwa speaks in the forest.
Biwa on the prairie.
Biwa in the city.
Biwa on the top of the mountain.
Biwa over the corn and beans
growing in green and golden rows.
Biwa rising like smoke.
Biwa makes us all of one flesh.

Biwa.
Biwa.
Biwa is a heap of ants
carrying grains of sound.
Biwa is the drum.
Biwa lifts water into the clouds.
Biwa cracks sticks of thunder.
Biwa is the drum.
Biwa is the drum.
Our coming here, Biwa traced
in the ground with a big stick:
mountains and gullies—the earth
remembers them.
A blanket over our head,
we grope our way.
You know how it is in the dark:
your body becomes fingers.
Biwa guides us,
saying: Learn this!
If you can't dance your own being
on the day of the weighing of souls,
no hope.
Death will suck the pith out of your very name.
Biwa told me this.
Biwa is the drum.
Biwa is the drum.

Biwa.
Biwa says it.
Single-eyed Biwa.
Biwa stands at the door of awakening.
Biwa.
Biwa comes walking out of the dawn
bearing platters of fruit.
Biwa naked.
Biwa jeweled.
Biwa with the sound of hearts.
Biwa.
Biwa.
Biwa the fountain.
Biwa bright knife.
Biwa thicket of sounds.
Biwa is the drum.
Biwa is the drum.
Biwa.
Biwa told me:
Fear not.
Biwa goes before.
Biwa beckons.
Biwa stands at the door of awakening.
Biwa carries dreamers.
Biwa is the drum.
Biwa rich brocade.

Biwa texture.
Biwa basket-weaver.
We are the basket.
Biwa is the drum.
Biwa is the drum.
Biwa is the drum.
Biwa says it.
It is so.

Wherever You Are

Wherever you are
you may close your eyes
and wonder
"Who breathes this breath for me?"

Your chest rises and falls
with the sureness of the tides.
The seas love the moon
and heave themselves up to be near her.

Now in the dark light of your inner world
the moon comes in her canoe
and offers to ferry you
across the black lake.

Whorls of water, slick as lacquer,
curl around the paddle
whose dips ripple the vast silence,
mother of all sound.

The eye of death
who sees us all
is like a mist
through which you pass.

Your prow nudges the sands
of the other shore.
Suddenly you are wherever you are
but in a different way.

O Lord and Lady

O lord and lady of infinite name,
in the stillness of my heart you call me to beauty.
The saffron and magenta feathers of sunset,
the liquid yearning of the flute—
these are the low branches of fir trees
that I part with my hands
to see more deeply into your meadow,
where, O mysterious one,
you give birth within me again and again.

Black Stone

Though born of our mothers,
we come from another place.
Black stone take me home.

And our dreams are root threads
reaching towards inner space,
O disk of black stone.

We've crawled through a tunnel
shaped like the dwindling bong of a bell,
Black stone take me home,

that leads from the ocean of life,
the waters eternal,
O disk of black stone.

Whenever the mouth of that tunnel
once again kisses our breast,
Black stone take me home,

we stand at the hub of the wheel
and everything's blest,
O disk of black stone.

How happy the one who knows
how to follow a course,
Black stone take me home,

with a compass of mystical journey
back to the source,
O disk of black stone.

But the way is a wilderness animal
who stares and then takes sudden flight,
Black stone take me home,

leaving its hoof prints or paw prints
glowing like embers at night,
O disk of black stone.

Come to me, tame me,
teach me the path to your spring.
Black stone take me home.

With patience I'll stalk you,
whatever each moment brings,
O disk of black stone.

O piece of the cud of time,
familiar with grief,
Black stone take me home,

carry me down past shafts of sunlight
to the floor of belief,
O disk of black stone,

there to read by firelight
the scriptures of my true home,
Black stone take me home,

painted with blood and earth on the walls
of the caves inside my bones,
O disk of black stone.

A lifetime of healing beauty,
a path like the rainbow's arc,
Black stone take me home,

is to spend each moment
this mysterious coin of the dark,
O disk of black stone.

Shape-shifting

With my third eye open
I bend the luminous threads of being,
my skin becomes as lustrous as a liquid pearl,
electric snakes of saxophone libido
slither through jazz tunnels
of shiny polished chrome
while waves of rainbows
are breaking on the shores of bliss;
Fierce jaws gape
at the mouth of each level,
and I slide through their darkness
wearing only the feathers of rhythm.

Winter Solstice 2003

It's not alone the embers of the dying year
but the sense of darkness falling everywhere,
and pooling shadows—the helping hand
grown grasping or become a punching fist,
cankers on the torn and plundered land,
the crass and ugly taken as the best.

Now seekers ask the endless, watchful night:
Where is the present source of living light?
Exhausted, used, we gather at the fire,
watch the flickering flames and see
into the glowing hearts of coals that murmur
in their red language and grow gray.

Deep within the heart there lies a seed
that can crack and open if the need
be great, as in the presence of a portal
in or out of life—a death, a birth,
a hurt or loss that tells us we are mortal,
the velvet dart of love, this wondrous earth.

If disconnected from our kin, creation,
the seed becomes a cup that fills with poison;
but, connected, fills and flows with nectar
from the web of life. Clearly
the mystery of the ever-present this
that never comes again holds us dearly.

This humble, human, earthly heart of hearts—
this is the place that recognizes darkness
and is itself a portion of the light—
the inner porthole to a blazing brilliance
encompassing both day and darkest night.

This time of outer darkness points within
and recalls us to our job that's always been
to blossom like a cherry tree in spring
with consciousness to benefit all life,
to bear our share of darkness with our light
and find the dawning hidden in the night.

First Encounter

You came in the night,
your mask shining
with mother of pearl, polished turquoise,
red coral and jet—
round and opulent
as the full moon.

Your glance
poured through me.
I felt the whole cord of my life—
all the way
from where you are spinning it
to where you shall cut it—
the whole cord throb
like a plucked string.

That one note
shook me awake.

And I have been trying to sing it
ever since.

In the Pine Forest

In the pine forest
touched with slight snow,
in the cabin
while winds whirl outside,
the fire in the fireplace
snaps its yellow fingers
and points at the invisible
where the essence of the wood goes
while its body powders to ash.

As we grow older,
glimpses come more and more often—
an arrowhead found in the dirt,
a chance illuminating phrase,
a love that seems to touch
the marrow of the universe.
We watch the ashes fall through the grate
and know our own will follow.
A strange and comforting music fills the heart
as we remember the vow
our soul has made
in that other place.

Love & Work

Páho

The prayerstick called páho
is two sticks—male and female—
side by side.
Honored equally,
different from each other,
each stands on its own
but not alone.
One stick made from two—
the cotton cord of life
binds them both together
beneath the feather
of the Great Mysterious.

Just so would I be with you,
my twin and equal,
bound together with the cord of life.
Yours is the face
I've always seen
behind the ones of everyone I've ever loved.
It's not the face of photographs
or mirrors,
but the face reflected
from your inner sacred spring;
where the heart is an instrument of music

and four stones of turquoise
draw an echo
from the temple inside.

Here is the cornmeal of our bodies;
Here is the pollen of fertility;
Here the love
of the male-and-female person
who created us—
It is a drop of honey.
All these wrapped in a cornhusk
tied between us, stick and stick.

The herb of summer's heat,
the herb of healing—gifts of the wild earth—
the man, the woman,
all bound together with the cord of life
beneath the feather of the Great Mysterious.
A piece of cord left dangling—
long cord means long life—
and at its end, the spirit breath
of eagle down.

There is no other I would come together with,
for I have always loved you.
Let us be a prayer together
while our feet remain on earth.
And when the elements have taken us
then let the beauty be unbounded.
Come to me. Find me.
I search for you.

The Man and the Woman

The man is a cottage
and the woman is a tree beside the door.
The man is a rock in a boulder field
and the woman is snow, melting.

He worships beauty
and wants to make all good things fruitful.
She is the daughter of Spoon Woman.
Her lap is fragrant and soft as tundra.

Spoon Woman lives forever,
growing younger and older, older and younger.
He is learning to dig a pit,
and pour blood into it, and weep.

When Spoon Woman is older
her face is like bark
and her hair is where the river has eaten its bank away
leaving matted and tangled roots.

When Spoon Woman is younger
she is vanilla
and a newly washed cotton nightgown,
sweet from drying in the sun.

He is the son of the One Who Starts Things Up.
Jumped by the Grizzly Man,
meeting the Dream Man,
he carves stone arrowheads
and makes pictures in the sand.

Talk to the stars now.
She says: Mother, Grandmother.
He says: Father, Grandfather.

When the man and the woman meet,
each one asks:
"What sound is this person today?"

Today he is the song of the barn swallow
and she is soft rain weaving a sash on the pond.
Tonight
he is the sound of a coyote's paw digging in snow,
she the sound of an acorn sprout
pushing through the damp earth.

In their bed
the two of them sleep
curled about each other.
And that spiral
winds through the whole world.

I Watch Your Body

I watch your body sleeping next to mine
and I see a river coursing through the night:
on a tray of black lacquer
a brushstroke of quicksilver
sweeps out under the clear moon.

Here on the riverbank
my moon is a pale drumhead.
Drum-a-drum, drum-a-drum,
the flat of my hand thumps
a small gold chain into the great night
to be eyes for me:
Towards where are you flowing?
And from what deep source
                far in the hills?

Baking

I love the smell of bread
when you and I are baking.
I love the feel of springy dough,
the kneading and the making.
But most of all I love the taste
which always is surprising.
Your oven's warm, I slip it in,
and oh the ecstasy of rising!

In the Cradle of the Morning

In the cradle of the morning
we lie in bed,
arms and legs interfolded
like the petals of a rose.
Our nakedness,
through which we became so shyly familiar,
has become the emblem of a nakedness
now far deeper
which we know in each other
without even speaking.

My hand rests on your ripening belly
and we feel this new one valiantly swimming
its nine-month voyage
out of the deep mystery.
Now we are saying words
as old as human speech,
and feeling urges that we share
with sister fox and mother bear
to have a place that's safe for kit or cub.
We feel life play us as its music.
Through our loins
goddess and god have touched,
and we lie amazed
in the wake of their eternal greeting.

My Newborn Son, Crying at 3 AM

I am not happy to report this, but soon after my son was born I met the axe-murderer living inside me. He has the body of a man but a mind that is a little ball of self-comfort, like a ball of yarn or a sleeping kitten spring-loaded with knives—greedy, razor-sharp, quivering.

Of all the inner beings this one lives in a crack in a rock, gives off no heat, and moves by oozing, except when prodded. Then it snaps. This part of me is probably about as mature as my one-week-old son is. It is also as ancient as rock. And I know that the rage here is like the binding energy of atoms, somehow fundamental to the universe, because it serves the will to survive. But how terrifying when the image of its release slashes across my inner screen: The atom splits, Hiroshima vaporized.

I remember that the first crime in the Oedipus story is not the son killing the father but the father abandoning the son. The father doesn't want to die; and the son carries the father's mortality. I lose sleep this week; I lose access to my wife, and the axe-murderer rouses, smelling death nearby. This is how it is when the temperature of the soul nears absolute zero. And this is a gift that my son has already given me: a look deep inside where I always hope to find gold, and a clear glimpse of the lead.

Western Lullaby

The man in the mountain is watching the sky.
There's sunlight and moonlight and stars riding high.
He's old as the stone and he's younger than rain
and he knows what they're feeling
when little ones cry.

The man in the mountain is an old Indian guide.
Two Moons is his name, and with you he'll ride
across valleys and mountains and forests and plains
to the sweet dreams awaiting
beyond the divide.

With bison and beavers and bears by your side
over diamond star snowfields your ponies will stride.
Sweet sagebrush and pine trees put wings on the air
so your friends can all join you
beyond the divide.

Now cellar doors open, tree roots reach deep,
and whales sing to sailors at sea.
Beyond the divide, take with you to sleep
love from your mommy and me.

And when you awake to the song of a lark
you'll bring back a gift from the shades of the dark.
Have no fear of the Not-Things, they're silly you'll see.
They're just bubbles that burst
when you smile in your heart.

So set your canoe on the river so wide.
Close your eyes, drift along, to the ocean you glide.
Two Moons has the paddle; he'll steer your way through
the great rainbow gateway
beyond the divide.

For My Son, On His Naming Day

Where your trail through life will lead you
I cannot say.
And some day for you I will be
a mere voice in your memory,
a few lines on paper.
But whatever comes,
I wish you to know these things:
First, that your mother and I love you
as true as water.
May love buoy you up
on all your difficult crossings.
Second, there is suffering in this world.
Those who will wound you
point their blade at some terrifying darkness
of their own, and stab through you
only by accident.
No blame.
Deep in that wounding
lurks your own shadow,
the thing that makes you round.
Examine your wounding,
water it with tears.
When you leave to find your wholeness,
as you must, know

that your life energy
has stubborn and enduring roots
through parents and grandparents,
through the ancient ones.
Trust the Great Mystery.
Know that in every moment
there is a door of truth and love
the size of the eye of a needle
that opens onto the next true moment.
May you be skilled, wise; may you
be humble and brave enough
to live in harmony with all beings,
even to a single blade of grass,
so that each door opens in beauty around you
for all the days of your life.
May your gifts flourish
for your joy
and the blessing of all.

After Swimming

I hold my five-year-old son
on my lap,
wrapped in his terry cloth towel
to cuddle away the goose bumps.

My head touches his
as I watch him
carefully nibble
the cinnamon-sugared graham cracker
in chosen bites.

Wordlessly
we admire
the timeless afternoon sun
sparkling
in golden bits of sugar.

Saturday Morning

later than usual—
our son has let us sleep.
Out in the living room
sprawled on the floor
very quietly he is playing
a game of checkers

                    with his eagle puppet.
The eagle is winning.

Watching this, I see how it is:
each of us, proud of his pupil.

First Light

The first light I see each day
comes from your face—
sometimes rosy as the drowsy clouds of dawn,
sometimes beaming at me
when I open my eyes.
In these few moments
as dreams trickle away
and before our work calls us to rise,
the whole universe
fits between two clean sheets
which we have sweetly rumpled.
You press your hand to my heart.
Until I see you again
I shall be swimming far from shore.

Men's Affinity for Tools

"A good tool
will last your whole lifetime,
if you take care of it."
My father said this
as he handed me my first grown-up tool:
a pair of long-nosed pliers,
just like his but radiantly new.
I loved the heft of them,
the attack of the jaws as they came together,
how the part for cutting wires
clipped the shiny copper like soft butter,
making little wedges
where it clicked the wire apart,
how easily they could twist and turn
the bits of metal that had hurt my fingers.

"A good tool
will last your whole lifetime."
My dad's words lifted me
from the round island of a child's thinking
and set me down on a strange path
stretching from the far distance
to my own two feet.

I hold those same pliers now,
darkened as his were then

by hand sweat and good use,
and I think of men's affinity for tools.
I have a doctor's tool,
the one thing left from the musty black bag
my grandfather gave me.
He said it was a hemostat—
little silvery pliers for human veins.
I think back through tunnels
on all the generations of men with their tools
to the great-grandfather of all men
with his sharp stone shaping something;
and on the huge satisfaction opening inside him,
the sense of relief
at guiding an urgent inner prompting
into a thing of weight and substance;
his gratitude to the stone;
how this man taught his son
the law of mastery: that a tool
gives skill to the hand as the hand grapples
with the awkwardness of the tool,
that every tool is a sort of lever
which pushes back
just as much as it pushes out
and molds a man

according to how it is used—
the hammer that builds well or poorly
gives to the inner dwelling the same quality;
that a man must listen through his tool
to the grain of things
and honor that,
or else become numb to his own life,
clumsy in a thick armor of tools.

"A good tool
will last your whole lifetime."
My father gave me
the great-great-grandson of that first sharp stone,
told me to take care of it
and in this way told me
to take care of myself,
wished me good life,
asked me to listen and to honor all things.

Pleasures of the Kitchen

The soft furry sound of water
coming to a boil . . .
Lifting the tender petticoats
of new lettuce fresh from the garden;
Peeling away the armor
from the warm smooth breast
of a hard-boiled egg;
Wandering blindfolded
through the harem of spices:
Cinnamon,
Cardamom,
Coriander,
Clove.

Putting an Onion Back in the Drawer

Its sibling had gone into the soup;
but I'd only needed one. Squatting
by the lowest drawer, suddenly I saw
this little globe in my hand—
this layered pearl of the dark earth,
its peeling outer paper skin red gold
as old copper, the under layer yellow beige
tinted pale green, watermarked
with darker meridians of longitude.
Its north pole the crushed and crackly remnant
of the stem that poked toward sunlight,
the south pole a tangled mass of root threads
like a badly sewn button.

A humble world citizen,
the onion is at home in every kitchen,
reminding us of sorrow when we cut it
and of that other tear-bringer: laughter.
We could not understand ourselves
nor savor depth so well without its necessary
metaphor—onion, union of many layers.
Like us it sweetens with a little cooking.
It swells its flesh in the dark

where sorrows ripen. But it is wise, not bitter.
It banishes blandness. Its deepest layer,
where it grows mysteriously,
is flame-shaped, like the flame
in the heart of every being.

Watering the Roots

My son, age ten,
is building a vehicle with his friend—
of scrap lumber, bent nails, and grand design.
Can I give advice? Yes.
Lend tools? Of course.
Everything I can possibly give
without swamping him.

I try to let him lead;
feel a surge of life pour through me
as I show him how to use
the brace and bit
I inherited from Abuelo,
to tell him how a ripsaw
differs from a crosscut
in words my Dad once said,
to snap a shiny half-inch socket
on the wrench for him
that in my hand had years ago
replaced my first car's clutch.

I remember Matt who coached me
on that work, and Dad and Abuelo,
and feel myself entering a stream
that flows from distant past
through me, my son, and endlessly away.

I smell sweet sawdust,
hear the ascending scale of tinks
as a nail is driven home,
see the vehicle take shape.
Already this son of mine is flowing away
and a new one comes,
and a new me.

Work Poem
(Green Gulch)

As we're helping to fence-in the upper pasture,
gray rain squalls roll through all day
giving us sunshine in low swells—
more than we've had for a week.

Good rain clothes keep us dry;
the mud squelches at our boots.
Using the banger to drop
            the metal stakes into the earth,
the lifting is heavy but good work.
The three of us are rolling through our tasks,
wrestling the heavy roll of fencing,
carefully twisting wires
with the fencing tool
so they don't snap off too twisted,
nailing U-nails to old posts green with lichen.
The whole field is green,
green the hillsides
            with the horses grazing
and green both up and down the valley.

We get to know that roll of fencing
like a story
as we unroll it.
The roll is lighter as the rest stands up in line.
The man comes by to check our work.
"I see you've done some fencing today," he says.

Walking in for lunch across the pasture,
there, like a candle blazing in a green night:
a single purple iris.

Some Events

Some events
have long lives.

Nearly forty years ago
having just learned to drive
I had the car alone
on a back road,
came up fast over a little rise
saw a box turtle crossing
felt the bump, heard the crunch,
before my brain could think of swerving.
I remember driving on,
my stomach sickened.

Now it's about time
I pull over, stop
and say a prayer
to bless that turtle
on its interrupted journey,
thank it for saving other lives—
perhaps including my own—
because of the space
it opened
under my own shell.

Like Two Trees

Here we are, growing old together like two trees
whose roots intermingle, whose leaves
caress each other in the breeze.
Holding you at night I settle into your gravity;
every cell of my body relaxes utterly.
You are better than dreams.
You are the sea with its depth.
I love the salt of your wetness,
the bruise of your lips, how you can lift
and skim me along your curling surf.
No matter how you age, your beauty
is as perfect as a circle.
And your will is an arrow flying
toward the highest good for all.
Treasure of my heart, when I look at you
I see the flowering light.
No words are needed.

Pebbles

Early morning—
the spider heeds her tensile web
beside the blushing river.

•••

In the long silence of drifting downstream
the lifted oar
drips.

•••

After studying the rapids
the far bank
swims upstream.

•••

The secret of the first half of life
is learning how to put on the sacred masks.
The secret of the second half
is learning to take them off again.

•••

How pregnant,
the undulant bodies
of water-polished stone—
their swelling curves,
their intimate folds.

• • •

Meeting an old friend
unexpectedly, I find
I have been holding my breath
                    for a long time.

• • •

Lady bug,
scaling the heights of a blade of grass—
I have seen you on the snows of glaciers
just as determined,
just as red.

• • •

Sitting in a wrinkle
        on the face of a god.
Mountains! Mountains!

• • •

Lightning flash—
a huge nerve of the air
suddenly bare.

● ● ●

The first flakes of winter snow—
Ah—
the skeletons of tears.

● ● ●

Hot flower of blue petals
burner of my camp stove—
tea soon
on this chill morning.

● ● ●

Autumn aspen:
saffron and lemon leaves,
graceful maidens, white skin—
a forest of standing rain.

● ● ●

In my bed
some summer nights
I stretch out for miles
like a blacktop desert highway
cooling off
beneath the stars.

• • •

Dandelions—
where the sun
has popped its buttons.

• • •

How intimate—
under the skirts of the night,
the pregnant moon!

• • •

Nighttime city puddles
where neon colors squirm
like jazz.

• • •

Warm evening.
Ten thousand ways
surf
crushes, crushes
against the shore.
You are as beautiful
as moonlight on the swirly water.

● ● ●

It is really very simple:
give everything.
and keep giving
until you are the whirling
of the turbines of the universe.

● ● ●

What time is it?
The shadow of the dead stem
is half-past the slickrock pothole.

● ● ●

Each moment
is so silent,
the net
soon fills with fish.

● ● ●

Late autumn,
two A.M.
I look out of my tent and think "Snow!"
but only an inch of moonlight has fallen.

● ● ●

Deep winter;
deep stillness in the forest.
The sun creeps down
and the slender lavender shadows
of the tree trunks
ski across the snow.

● ● ●

Awake at night
after a shameful dream—
Whose?

● ● ●

Gentle rain, all night
stars tapping
on my tent.

• • •

Plume of yellow smog—
I vow
to live lightly.

• • •

The heads of state
so often meet,
while hearts of state
so seldom do.

• • •

I see from above.
I see all around.
My song carries far.
Thank you.

• • •

After her shower,
comb through fine hair—
pines in the mist.

● ● ●

A fine meal always
looks different
from the other end
of the fork.

● ● ●

The hummingbird dips her slender bill,
the whole universe
pivots.

● ● ●

Like snowflakes softly ticking down—
our constant clean arrival
at this present moment.

● ● ●

In selflessness
great things form
as large numbers swarm with zeroes.

● ● ●

I arrange small sticks for a fire;
but the flame arrives
on an unseen hand
from out of the clouds.

● ● ●

Sandy bottom of the mountain pool—
shadows somehow fallen
through the rippling golden net.

Piñon

desert piñon—
needles glinting
in the sun

graceful piñon—
dancing
with the seasons

solitary piñon—
the moon slipping through
its fingers

Meditations on Stones

On the steppingstones of days
we cross the great stream.

Stones are sanctuaries
in which time is a well-kept secret.

Envy: the stone in the belly.

Raindrops
on a sun-warmed stone—
fragrance!

Each stone—
just the right shape.

Listen—
the prayers that stones make
in the stream.

A Little Night Poem

May your sleep be as sound
as a bean's underground,
May you wake
as a sprout to the light.
The blossom will come
in the rain and the sun
and its roots
will be here in the night,
the night;
its roots
will be here in the night.

About the Author

Chris Hoffman is a poet, ecopsychologist, and consultant. His poems have appeared in national journals including *Appalachia*, *The Christian Science Monitor*, *Sea Kayaker*, *Sufi Journal*, and *The Chrysalis Reader*, as well as in the anthology *The Soul Unearthed*. He enjoys performing his work both solo and in music and dance collaborations. In addition to his other poetry book, *Realization Point*, Chris is the author of *The Hoop and the Tree: A Compass for Finding a Deeper Relationship with All Life*, a book on ecopsychology and native wisdom.

Chris has taught ecopsychology at Naropa University and has delivered many workshops and presentations on applied psychology. As a consultant Chris has facilitated human and organization development in a variety of business, educational and therapeutic settings. He currently specializes in organizations working for a sustainable future. He is a licensed professional counselor.

Chris is a long-time student of Zen and T'ai chi and is interested in traditional healing practices and sacred dance. His wilderness experience includes backpacking, mountaineering, and river running. He lives with his wife in Boulder, Colorado. They have one son. (More information at www.hoopandtree.org)